Magical Unicorn
DOT-TO-DOTS

Natasha Rimmington

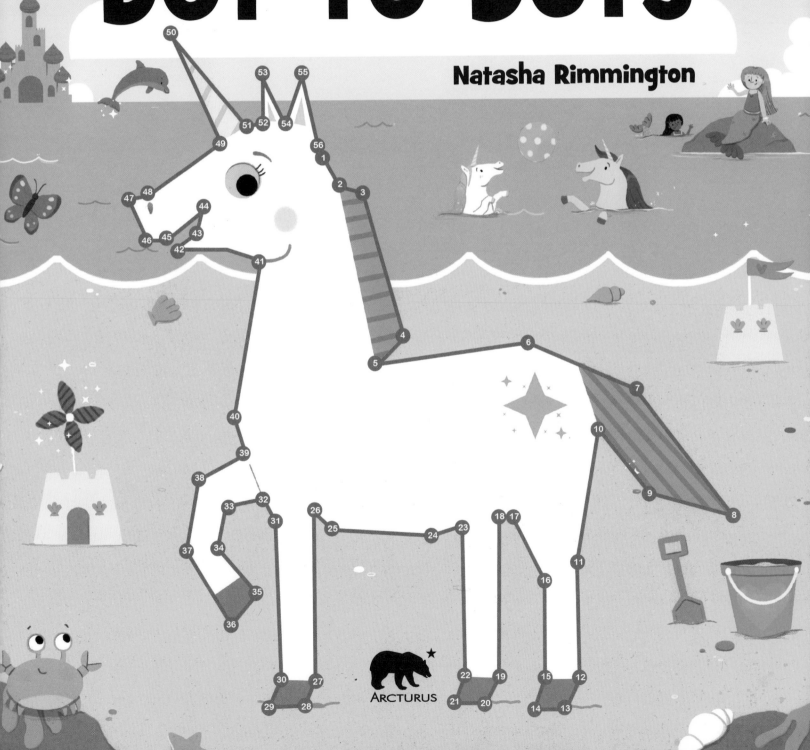

ARCTURUS

This edition published in 2019 by Arcturus Publishing Limited
26/27 Bickels Yard, 151–153 Bermondsey Street,
London SE1 3HA

Edited by JMS Books llp with Sebastian Rydberg
Layout by Chris Bell
Illustrations by Natasha Rimmington

ISBN: 978-1-78950-485-9
CH007030NT
Supplier 29, Date 0719, Print run 9323

Printed in China

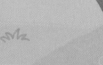

Welcome!

Let's go on a magical dot-to-dot adventure!

3

Picnic Time!

Buttercup and Moonbeam are having a picnic in the woods.

Manny Monkey wants Buttercup's picnic basket!

4

Moonbeam loves a slice of cake!

5

At the Fair

Unicorns love a day at the funfair!

The fairies are enjoying the merry-go-round.

6

Dapple loves mint chocolate chip ice cream.

7

Under the Sea

It's time to head to the beach.

These pretty mermaids can breathe underwater.

Marigold can swim, but she needs to use a snorkel!

Fun at the Beach

Which sandcastle has won first prize?

1st PRIZE

Moonbeam's castle is the winner today.

It's Spa Day!

The fairies are very busy in the salon.

Moonbeam likes to keep her mane looking smart.

12

Fairies like to paint their nails "fairy pink"!

13

There are so many different animals to adopt.

Will Una choose a cute little ginger kitten?

Harvest Time

The red apples are ripe and ready.

24 1

23

4

19 22

18

21 3 2

6

20

17 5 7

16

15

8

14

9

13 11 10

12

The fairies
pluck apples
off the tree.

Clover the Unicorn
eats them all!

17

Sweet Dreams!

Buttercup and Moonbeam are at a sleepover.

The naughty fairies are having a pillow fight.

18

They are keeping
the sleepy unicorns
wide awake!

Over the Rainbow

Starlight and Dancer have wings.

Watch them gallop through the clouds.

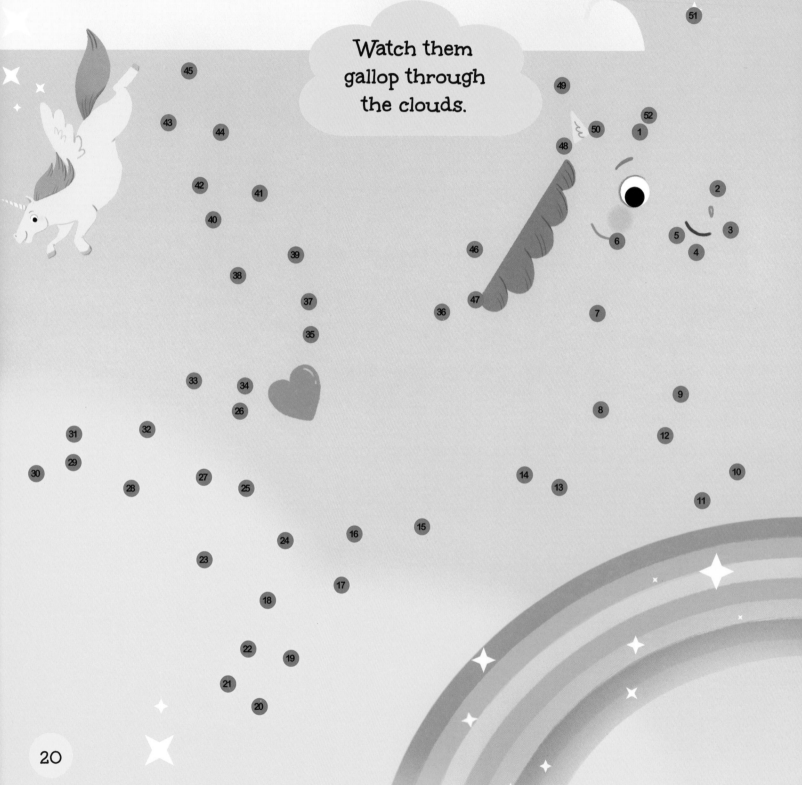

They are playing chase.

Fairy Cakes

It's baking day in the busy kitchen.

Acorn is serving his pretty cupcakes.

22

The fairies are using bright pink frosting.

23

Hidden Treasure

What have the
mermaids found?

Look at the
sparkly jewels
and pearls.

30
31
33
21
32
29
34
20
23
24
5
22
28
35
25
19
4
26
6
18
27
36
8
17
37
7
2
3
16
9
1
11
45
10
46
38
12
15
44
41
39
47
43 42 40
13 14 48

There are gold and silver coins, too.

Volleyball!

It's a truly magical match.

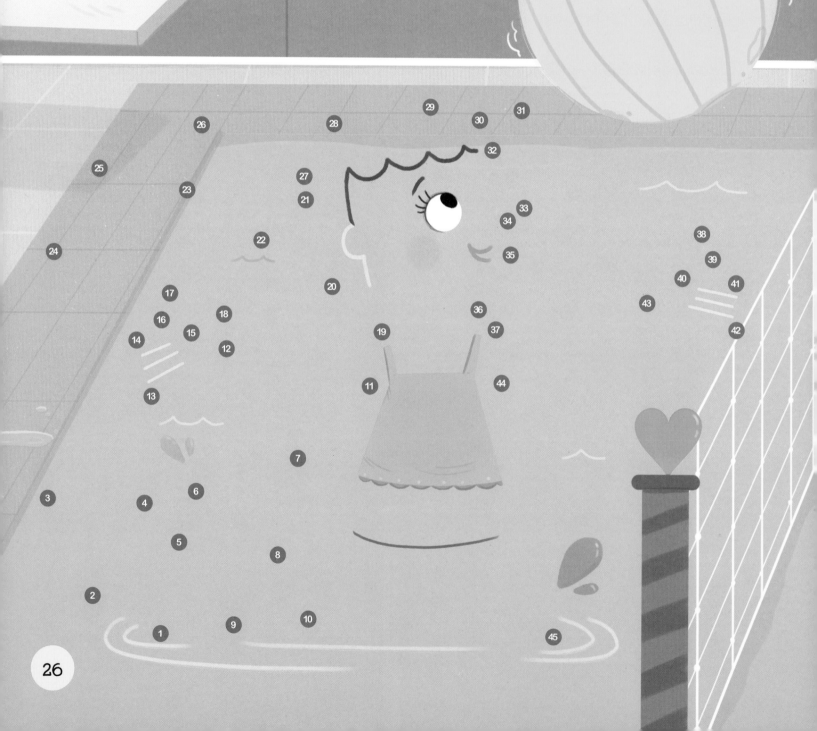

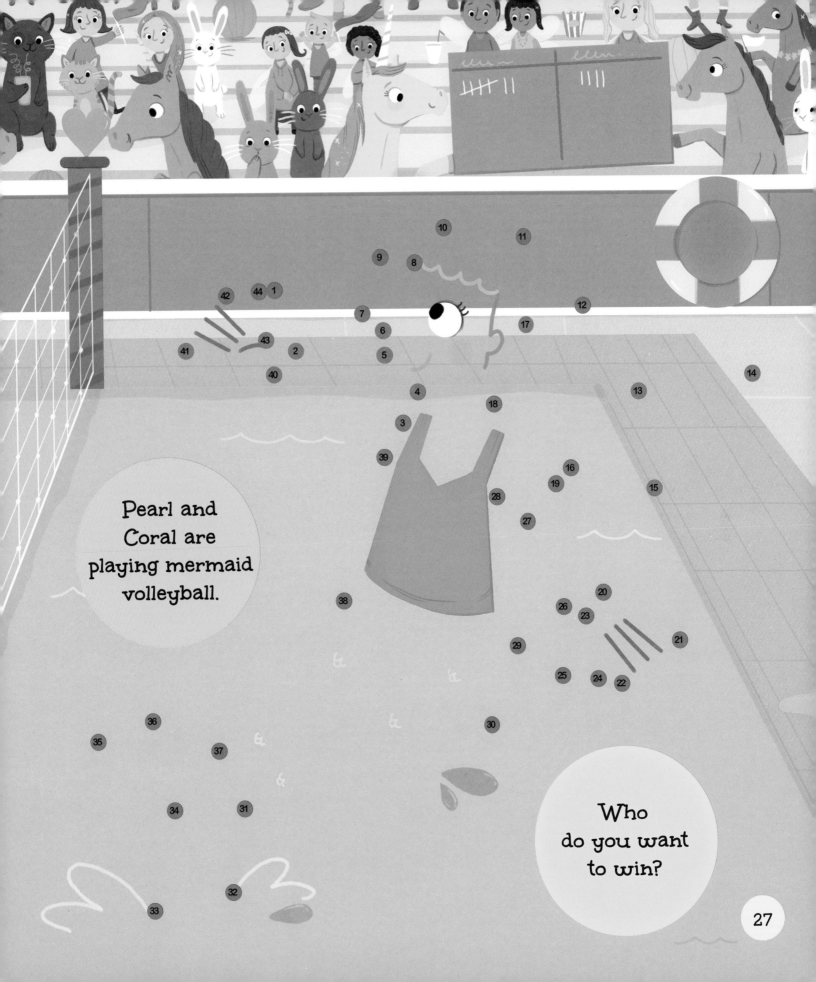

Pearl and Coral are playing mermaid volleyball.

Who do you want to win?

Art Class

Did you know that unicorns can paint?

Look at the beautiful butterfly.

It looks real enough to fly away!

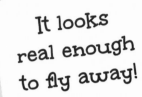
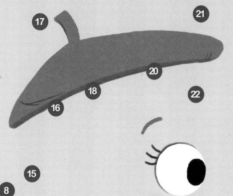

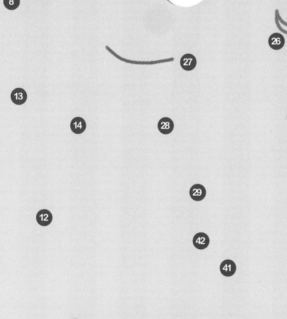
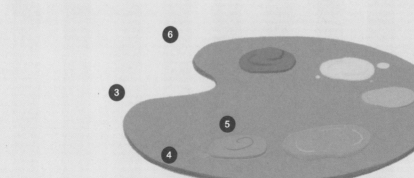

Firefly Hunt

These tiny insects glow in the dark.

Acorn collects fireflies with his net.

Blossom sets them free again.

6
7
4
5
8
43
9
3
44
2
12
10
14
1
15
13
11
41
45
16
42
17
20
47
21
19
46
22
18
48
23
25
24
26
50
49
40
39
34
38
35
28
36
33
27
29
32
37
30
31

Birthday Party

Hip, hip, hooray!

9   10

12

7

8   11   13

6   19   20

5   21

4   15   14   22

3   2   18

16   17   23

1   24

There are so
many parcels
to open.

There are lots of candles to blow out.

33

Snowball Fight

The world has turned white overnight!

Moonbeam and Blossom are playing together.

Snowballs fly through the air.

Hide-and-Seek

The sun is shining in the park.

What is little Kitty hiding under?

23
24 27
22 28
25 31
26 32
29 35
30 36
33 1
34

3
4 2
21
20 18
17
19 16 14
13
15 12 10
9
11 8 6
7

Where has Moonbeam decided to hide?

37

Ice Cream Cafe

Sunday is the day for ice cream sundaes!

Look at all the cherries and cream.

The unicorns are counting the sprinkles on their desserts.

39

Beauty Salon

It's pampering day for pets.

Kitty loves having her fur brushed.

41

Tea for who?

It's lovely weather for a tea party in the garden.

43

Ice Rink

It's time to get your skates on!

Starshine needs two pairs of skates.

Fairy Bluebell only needs one pair.

45

Winter Fun

It's snowing again!

Let's slide down the slippery slopes.

Watch out for the snowman!

47

Flower Fairies

Would you like to meet a flower fairy?

They live in the tallest sunflowers.

They also live in tulips and tiny daisies.

49

Fairy Boutique

Who has the best dress?

Bella's dress is as red as a rose.

Blossom's is as blue as the sky.

51

Adventure Park

Look who has come out to play today.

Manny Monkey
hangs upside
down.

Who is climbing up to help him?

53

Time to Fly

Kites come in many shapes and sizes.

Some have many pretty bows.

Others look like flying flowers.

55

Lakeside Larks

Unicorns know how to have fun!

Dancer is swinging from a big tree.

Sunny is fishing from a small boat.

57

Fairy Wish

Some wishes do come true.

43   45   46

35

44

34   41   39   47   48

42   49

40   50

38   51

33

37   52

31   53   3

32   36   4

54   2   6

28   1   5

30   10   8   7

29   9

27   11

26

24   25   20

19

22   21   13

17   18   12

23

15   14

58

16

Fairy Rose throws a coin into the fountain.

Will the unicorn grant her wish?

Cupcake Contest

Which cupcake will win the prize?

Will it be the one with the candles?

24 · 25

18 · 19

22 · 23 · 26

21

27

31 · 32

20

28

29

30

17

16

33

34

15

37 · 38 · 36

35

14

39

13

12

40

41

4

10

8 · 7 · 6

11

9 · 5

1

2

3

Or the funny bunny cake with the stars?

61

Sparkle is good at cycling.

62

Wheely Good!

Who can go the fastest?

Shimmer prefers to scoot along.

Unicorns are very good at balancing books.

Library

It's reading time at school.

They don't need satchels!

65

A Magical Visit

Today is a very special day.

Cherry is off to meet her friends.

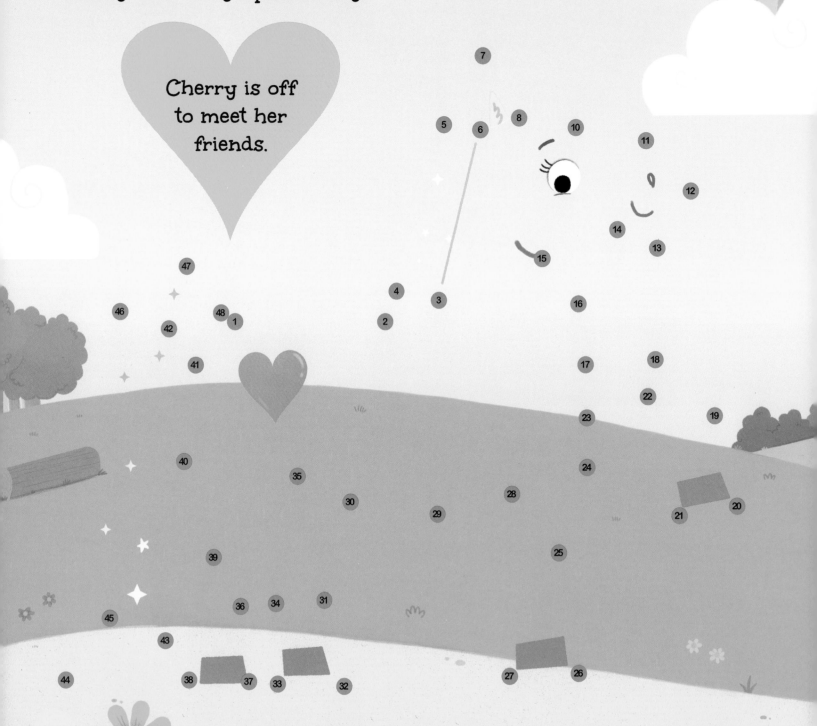

66

They live in
a fairytale
castle.

67

Pool Party

It's cool by the pool.

69

Picture Perfect

Who's having fun in the photo booth?

Unicorns love making silly faces.

They also like dressing up in crazy clothes.

Waterfall Pool

The water rushes down from way up high.

It lands with a very loud splash.

Can you see the fish in the pool?

73

Stars from the Sky

Snowflake fairies are artists.

They paint millions of snowflakes.

Each flake is like a tiny, twinkling star.

75

Milkshake Bar

Bubble, bubble, fairy trouble.

Rosa loves strawberry shakes.

Daisy and Grace prefer orange.

Water Sports

See who's having fun in the sea.

Mermaids and dolphins love to play together.

Dolphins enjoy jumping out of the water.

Bluebell can juggle lots of balls in the air.

Buttercup can balance a ball on her nose.

Circus Tricks

It's time to learn some new skills.

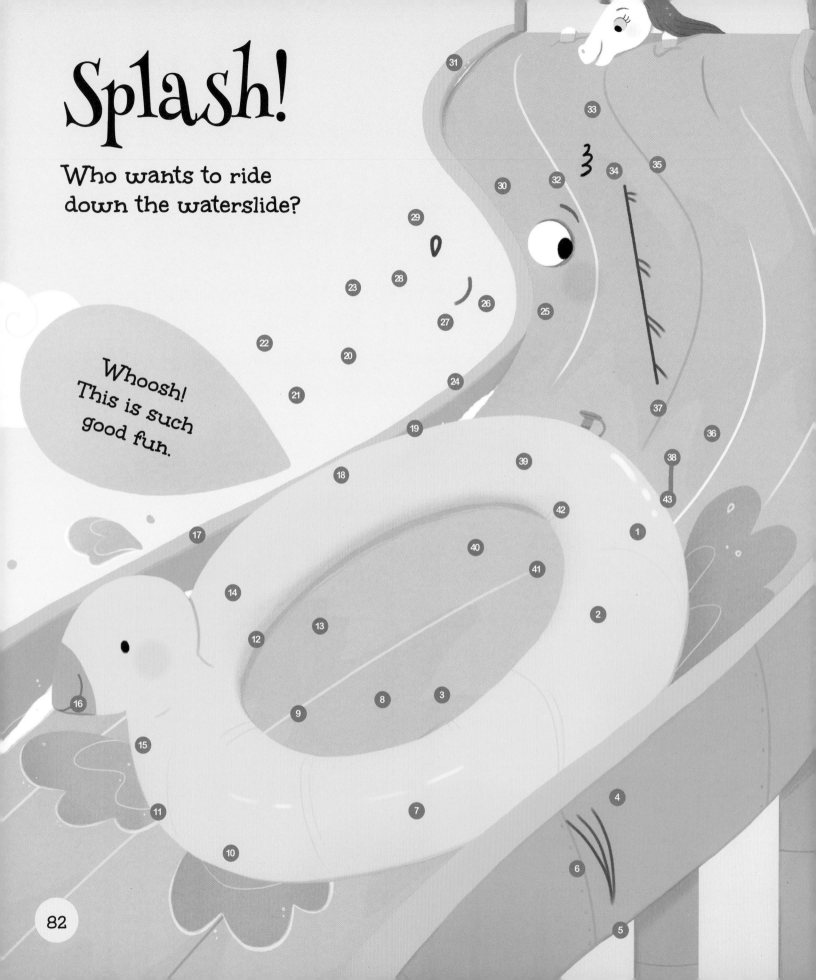

Splash!

Who wants to ride down the waterslide?

Whoosh! This is such good fun.

82

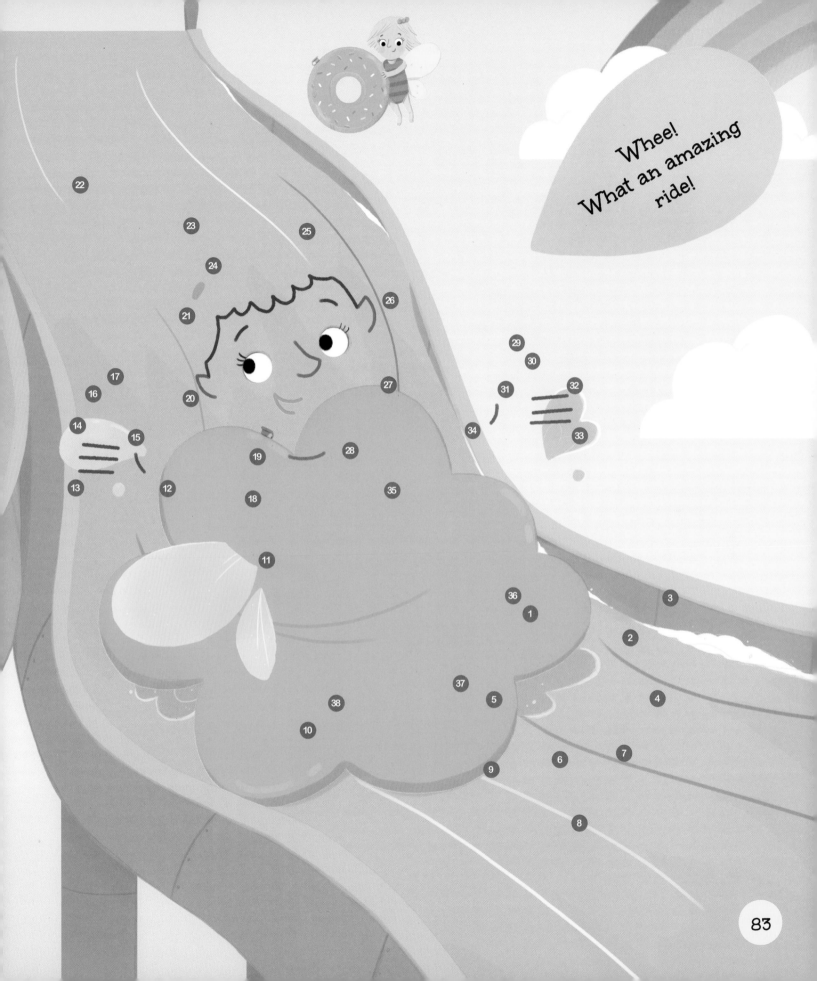

In the Garden

Growing plants is like magic.

Fairy Foxglove is planting the seeds.

Treetop House

Wouldn't it be lovely to live in a wood?

You could sleep high up in the trees.

Fairies might drop by for magical picnics.

Tug-of-war

The fairy games have begun.

Will the unicorns be stronger?

Or will the fairies use their powers?

89

Arctic Adventure

Unicorns and narwhals both have horns.

They love to tell each other stories and jokes.

Solutions

On the following pages we show you what was hidden in the pictures. Once you have connected the dots, your drawings should look just like these.

Page 3

Pages 4-5

Pages 6-7

Pages 8-9

Pages 10-11

Pages 12-13

Pages 14-15

Pages 16-17

Pages 18-19

Pages 20-21

Pages 22-23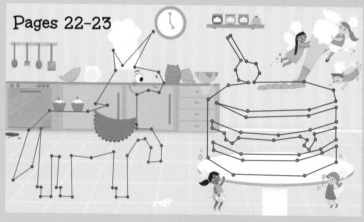

Pages 24-25

Pages 26-27

Pages 28-29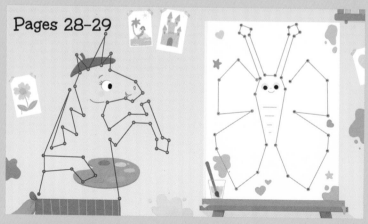

Pages 30-31

Pages 32-33

Pages 34-35

Pages 36-37

Pages 38-39

Pages 40-41

Pages 42-43

Pages 44-45

Pages 46-47

Pages 48-49

Pages 50-51

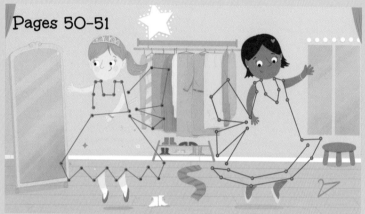

Pages 52-53

Pages 54-55

Pages 56-57

Pages 58-59

Pages 60-61

Pages 62-63

Pages 64-65

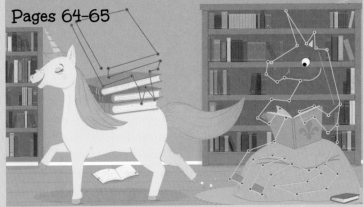

Pages 66-67

Pages 68-69

Pages 70-71

Pages 72-73

Pages 74-75

Pages 76-77

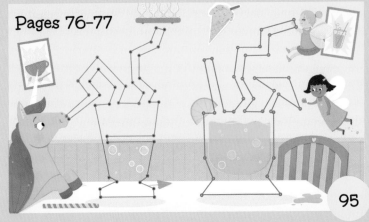

Pages 78-79

Pages 80-81

Pages 82-83

Pages 84-85

Pages 86-87

Pages 88-89
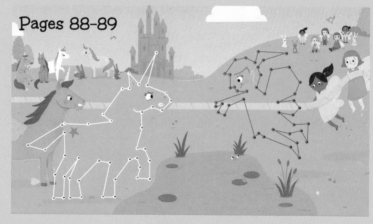

Page 90